THE ULTIMATE HANDGUNNER

ALL-NEW METHODS OF HANDGUN EFFICIENCY AND ACCURACY

plus

FOR WOMEN:
GUN SELECTION & DEFENSE TECHNIQUES

by

Cal Highway Patrol Rangemaster David B. Smith
&
Army SF Sgt. Don Paul

Don Paul is a former Green Beret who became a writer after his parachute failed on a mission over Panamanian jungles in 1976. Find a more complete bio and ten other books plus free outdoor tips at Don's website: **www.survival-books.com**

Well-published in numerous gun magazines, Dave spent his career with the California Highway Patrol. He's taught many officers how to place bullets accurately and has reloaded a kazillion handgun bullets. I reverently call him a pistol range-rat. (He chews up targets).

AMDG. Ad Majoram Dei Gloriam
"To the major Glory of God"

I am now 78. You and I both know old guys drop every day. Judgement coming soon? I'm reading my Bible a lot lately and I see: 1) How God's way works in relationships to create harmony, peace and brotherly kindness. 2) How man's way doesn't work and creates dishonesty, jealousy, hatred, and crime, which gradually destroys a society (Ferguson, MO.) Christians try to succeed spiritually, but fail. Non-Christians decide to fail spiritually, and succeed. I wrote this book for handgun owners who don't want to become victims of those who've decided to fail. I thank God, and ask that I conform to His Word and Will as I write.

Prayer: *Lord, we're in Your Hands. As this book goes to publication, I rededicate everything I am to You. I am sorry that it took me so long to realize that the only thing ever to keep me alive and help me was Your Grace and Your Holy Bible. Amen.*

Library of Congress Catalog Card Number:
Publisher's Cataloging in Publication
Paul, Don, 1937-
    ULTIMATE HANDGUNNER, *All New Methods of Handgun Efficiency and Accuracy.* by Don Paul
        p. cm.
    Includes index & glossary.
    1. Wobble grid for handgun shooting practice. 2. Mix 'n Match handgun loading to extend range and power. 3. Guns for ladies. 4. Pistols for defense.

I. Paul, Don, 1937- II. Title
        HV   SAN   QBI

CONTENTS

CONTENTS
(cont.)

> Together, we have spent a combined century—over 100 years—in the gun world. Could we get together and teach you? One or both of us survived in the jungles, worked as a cop, taught others how to shoot, worked as a gunsmith, carried and fired every weapon, competed and won everything from trophies to medals, shot it out on the street, and read most everything printed about handguns. *It annoys us that nobody has taught what we consider to be so obvious.*
>
> See: numerous articles published in various gun magazines by DAVID SMITH.

ULTIMATE HANDGUNNER

CHAPTER 1
Why This Book?

As it stands right now:

1. Buyers choose handguns for the wrong reasons and often buy the wrong gun.

2. There has been no method to determine the size of your cone of fire at a distance. If your cone of fire is too large to hit a long distance target, don't take those shots. Why punch holes in the air?

Without grid information, gun buyers often purchase too much big caliber gun. That gun also goes bang and recoils excessively. It's heavy, difficult to carry, and unpleasant to shoot. It stays at home.

Without our wobble grid, errant trigger pull influence cannot be measured. Since our wobble grid provides a way to practice at home, you can discover your best shooting position, teach yourself perfect trigger squeeze, and learn sight alignment without spending money at a shooting range.

3. For both men and women, most new guns need to be improved and modified after purchase, especially the grip size. Few know how to add grips so the gun can be held correctly. That causes very creative shooters to pepper the landscape here, there and everywhere.

4. Of all the guns in the world right now, over 90% are loaded with only one kind of ammunition. THAT'S WRONG! A handgun needs to provide you with firepower for targets at various distances. Moreover, different bullets produce different results. You will be faced with soft and tough targets, short and long distances, and day and night shooting. Sometimes you need penetration (engine block) and at other times you need to be effective at long distance. Some commercial bullets will do more damage than others and often solve your problem.

If your handgun is loaded with only one kind of bullet that shoots at one distance with the same power, you can't solve long distance emergencies or short-range surprises. When that's the case, you don't need a gun as much as a Bible.

5. Incoming! You can find all kinds of material and opinions on how to shoot. But I have never seen any information on how to deal with incoming (someone shoots at you). The reason for owning a handgun is to defend against a marauder, who most likely is likewise armed with a handgun. How can you be so unprepared for what could easily happen?

At this writing, several police officers have been assassinated by a person who walked up to the police car's window and shot. If the police officer's handgun is in his holster it's difficult to draw. I suggest a new law: Illegal to approach car within ten feet. Show of empty hands required. Officer policy is to draw and be ready to fire if person crosses buffer zone without getting permission or showing empty hands

See CONQUER CRIME (PAUL). Reference: gun to be concealed in purse and shot through leather at attacker.

Dave and I put our brains, shooting ability and NEW IDEAS together to bring you information never before in print. To the list above, we add methods you need to use to become a super shooter.

THREE ROADS TO SHOOTING PERFECTION

To create a truly phenomenal shooting result, you need:

1. shooter improvement,
2. gun modification, and
3. ammo improvement. In other words, buy this weapon, improve it this way, buy various kinds of ammunition and out-shoot every other gun out there.

LEARN TO DETECT WOBBLE

We think you'll agree that our wobble system is the most important shooting world discovery in modern times. That's because it analyzes and then gives you the solution to many causes of poor marksmanship.

A. Nothing is more innovative or important than measuring the amount of natural shake (wobble) you exhibit when you aim. THE WOBBLE GRID measures your bullet placement ability in MOA (Minutes Of Angle). The measurement tells you precisely at what distance you can hit.

B. Setting up and using the system can be done at home. You don't have to burn gunpowder. The system cuts your ammunition cost substantially.

C. The grid enables you to analyze your marksmanship and make corrections to your shooting technique.

D. It helps you discover the reason(s) you shoot an occasional "wild shot."

Copy the page on which we drew the graph and work on different handgun shooting positions while you note how much your wobble varies. In the past all we had to go by were the bullet holes you made in the target. But the essence of good marksmanship (or any other sport demanding physical performance) is in tracing error to cause. The shape of the wobble you produce on the grid enables you to correct your shooting position and grip so that your shooting accuracy improves drastically.

What else? The GRID teaches you trigger control! Listen to this. Almost everybody disturbs sight alignment when the hammer falls. Before the GRID, we didn't have a way to measure trigger error. With the naked eye, we dry fire, and it "looks" good. But, as if you could place the whole shooting sequence under a microscope, the wobble grid detects the smallest errors in the shooting process.

Without using our grid, there is no other way. This grid isolates and identifies the most frequent causes of poor marksmanship. Wrong focus on sights, trigger jerk, trigger finger not perpendicular to the line of pull, shift in grip because of recoil, etc. Once detected, you can correct them and thus eliminate marksmanship failure.

Bullets need to solve particular problems. To be effective, bullets need a certain weight, composition and structure (hollow point, for example).

DEALING WITH DANGER

People who want life-saving knowledge (cops and military forces) read gun literature in order to stay alive. Getting shot *at* is something few writers think about. However, when you fail to prepare, you prepare to fail. In gun talk, don't leave home half cocked. See our chapter on incoming.

The following chapters will teach you how to use any handgun you own now or will buy later so that your bullet placement achieves perfection.

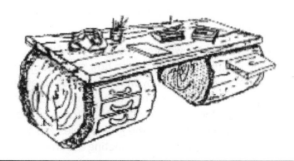

Desk appears in *GREAT LIVIN' IN GRUBBY TIMES. You can make all the furniture you need with a chainsaw.* Sold out as of Feb 16, soon to be re-written.

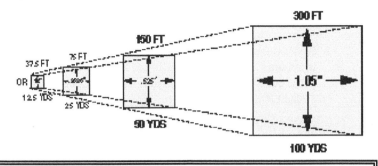

DETERMINE HITTING DISTANCE FROM WOBBLE

Every law enforcement officer in the country needs to measure his or her wobble. Wobble is always equal to a measurable cone of fire at any given distance. It dictates how far away you can shoot with accuracy. If you exceed that distance, your cone of fire will expand. A secondary problem occurs at long distance: The shooter tries to make it extra good, and therefore indulges in defective shooting. Jerk to get it just right when the sights are on.

It doesn't matter how far away you place the MOA wobble grid in determining what your wobble is. Just make sure the size of the grid matches the distance you use. At 25 yards, you need 1/4" squares.

Measure your wobble periodically. As you improve, your wobble will decrease so your assured shooting distance will increase.

ULTIMATE HANDGUNNER

CHAPTER 2
Our Wobble Grid

You become an expert marksman by eliminating all the causes of misses. You need to:

1. Learn to hold your handgun exactly the same way for every shot.

2. Aim your handgun precisely.

3. Cause trigger to act without disturbing the gun.

4. Follow through. Stay on target after firing.

To discover what causes a miss, ask, "What could go wrong when I pull this trigger?"

1. Sights were aligned the last time you looked, but misaligned when the bullet left the barrel. Your trigger finger needs to be in the correct position so that your trigger squeeze will be straight to the rear.

2. Sights were aligned—on target—with good trigger squeeze—but with no follow-through so the barrel moved during the shot.

3. Sights couldn't be aligned after dark.

4. The shooter was out of breath, or he was shaking. Shooter aimed at the whole target body rather than focusing on one small part of it, such as a belt buckle or nose. Reference Dave's favorite quote from the movie *The Patriot*: "Remember, aim at little, miss a little."

Sight misalignment makes bullets miss. I was a member of a high level Army Marksmanship Detachment and I heard this in the lectures to the troops over and over again: "To shoot well, you have to align your sights, and then cause the hammer to fall without disturbing your sight alignment."

As you know, your eye can only focus on one location. Shooting with metal sights requires that you focus on target, front sight, and rear sight. To do that best and most effectively, we have a focus sequence. All is correct when target and rear sight are out of focus but front blade is in focus. Then stare at that front sight while it sits in the middle of the rear sight with target in the background.

Now, squeeze the trigger so you don't make your barrel (sights) point somewhere else. The number one cause of missed handgun shots is faulty trigger squeeze, even if slight.

FUNDAMENTALS ARE CRITICAL

Use a code (mnemonic) word, "brass." Each letter stands for: Breathe, Relax, Aim, Squeeze, Surprise. Memorize the word(s) and go through the sequences each time you pull a trigger.

Breathe. Take in a deep breath, let about two thirds of it out, and then hold your breath while you shoot.

Relax. Hang the weapon loosely by your side. Concentrate on total relaxation. Not one muscle tense. Keep your finger off the trigger!

Aim. Adjust your body so that you point at your target naturally.

Close your eyes and point the weapon. Open your eyes. Shift your feet so that your natural shooting position moves your sights on target. Lower the weapon again, close eyes; raise weapon and point, then open eyes. You need to be on target; if not, re-adjust your standing position. Your goal: Be on target with zero muscle strain.

Now aim, but first recognize that the word "aim" has two parts.

A. Gun sight alignment. This is the most critical part of the aiming process. Focus on the front sight so it's placed perfectly in the rear sight notch. Ignoring wobble, begin to put pressure on the trigger. Stare at your front sight with the unfocused target in the background and the unfocused rear sight in the foreground. You need to see and concentrate on the sharp image of the front sight. Steadily increase pressure on the trigger until the hammer drops as a surprise.

Simply stare at the sights with your focus on the front blade. Squeeze. When the hammer drops, note any change in sight alignment. When your sights stay perfectly still after many hammer drops, your trigger finger is passing the straight-to-the-rear test.

B. Sight picture. The target must remain out of focus while the focus of your eyes remains fixed on the front sight. Many misses occur when shooter looks at the target. When the front sight is moved to "aim" at the target, the sights on the gun come out of alignment.

Squeeze—straight to the rear. If the trigger puller pushes the trigger to either side instead of straight to the rear, the round will fly off in the direction in which the sight alignment was disturbed. Result: a complete miss.

Surprise. If the gun doesn't fire as a surprise, the shooter knew when it would fire. How? Because the shooter's trigger finger made it happen, which, of course, sends the bullet in a weird direction.

GUN ACCURACY

Your handgun can be improved enough to place lead with precision. You can fire-lap the barrel with a NECO kit, change the sights, and work on the trigger. We call that "gun accuracy." It has nothing to do with shooting skill or super match ammunition—just the gun itself. Place the gun in a rest with no wind blowing, a perfect sight picture and a tender, steady and straight-to-the-rear trigger squeeze. Therefore, no outside influence can cause shot group spread. Result: You discover how the gun alone shoots.

7

> I wounded a bear once with a Ruger single action .357, 6" barrel. He came out of that tree after me! Fortunately, he got into a fight with the hounds (Vet bill was $600). How did "wounded" happen? Stock grips, so with a two-hand hold, I pushed the round a bit left. Buy new grips so your trigger finger gets positioned just right and pulls straight to the rear.

Handgun replacement parts are available to create match masterpieces. Modifications to automatic handguns can cause them to malfunction. "Mal" means bad. No big deal if you are punching holes in paper. But if "mal" happens in a gunfight, someone will be punching holes in you!

Blow back powers the slide to the rear and ejects a case. A new round loads. Maybe. Maybe not if you tighten the slide. Therefore, you pull your trigger on an empty chamber. After a quick draw, lightweight triggers often cause holey feet.

Ambidextrous safeties? I don't think so. Incidentally, it's imperative that your safety be positive. Whether on or off, you want it to stay that way until you change it.

Want a nightmare? Dream about a fire fight in which you can't shoot and you don't know why. What was the horror? You caught a long or protruding safety lever on clothing during the fight so your weapon was locked up on safe. Finally, big "mushroom" magazine release buttons can be fatal if you hit the button in the heat of combat.

With hand in open air (no gun), move the tip of your index finger straight to the rear. Watch it closely. If it moves either left or right, sideways pressure on the trigger creates a critical error.

OPERATIONAL ACCURACY...

Suppose you are 5' 10" tall. You purchase a .38 Special Ladysmith from Smith and Wesson. Great choice. But women who are tall normally have long fingers. The Ladysmith grips are small, and without bulkier grips, you won't be able to establish the correct hand-to-trigger posture. Long fingernails compound the situation and stick the palm to make it unbearable. Moreover, shoot just once and the recoil will shift the pistol in your hand. This is handgun disaster. Result: You start punching holes in the horizon.

DAVE WRITES: My dad knew an FBI agent who, during a fire fight, thought his assailant was in front of him. But the criminal germ surprised him by blasting into the room through a door from the agent's right. As he swung his weapon right to get his sights on the guy, he hit the cylinder release (revolver), which caused several cartridges to land on the floor.

DON SAW... at the recent SHOT SHOW. One company produced an auto with a magazine release on both sides of the gun. DANGER! Accidental magazine release can get you killed. Why make magazine release more available for shooters who need to shoot more... when apparently they couldn't hit anything from the first ammo load?

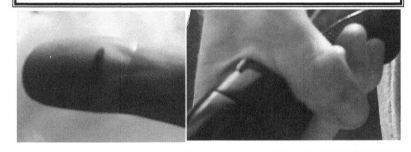

Left: Spot your trigger finger needs to touch the trigger—<u>every time</u>.

Right: That will happen automatically when you position a certain spot on the back of your pistol grip against the web of your thumb to forefinger. (Illustration from *SURVIVAL SHOTGUN*)

Many shooters don't know this. The function of grips on your handgun stock is to control the <u>consistent placement of your trigger finger</u>. **IT MUST BE PERPENDICULAR TO THE DIRECTION OF TRIGGER MOVEMENT.** If the grips are too large, your trigger finger will push the trigger to make you shoot horizontal groups off to the left. Grips too small? Finger will then wrap around trigger to pull muzzle right. The correct hand wrap around handgun grips is critical. When it's correct, reach trigger pull will be neither left nor right, but <u>exactly</u> to the rear.

NIGHT TIME IS WHEN ACTION OCCURS

Handgun shooting for real most often occurs when the perp or burglar comes in on you during the night. You're half asleep. Therefore, once you learn the basics of shooting, add advance instruction.

Think: When am I most likely to require the aid of gunpowder? Answer: At three AM. Because of this, learn to shoot instinctively. It's easy to point at anything with your upper forearm bone (radius). The key to successful shooting in the dark is to make sure the barrel of your handgun is in line with your forearm! That way, wherever your forearm points, a bullet is sure to follow.

Now, in absolute darkness, shoot. Feel the recoil? If the recoil is not in line with your forearm:

    a. You may experience some discomfort, or pain.

    b. the recoil will move your forearm to one side or the other.

You don't have to look at your arm-to-gun-barrel relationship. Feel it. When the weapon fires and moves your shooting arm either slightly left or right, keep practicing until you feel the jolt of recoil directly in line with your forearm.

BULLET PLACEMENT ERROR DISCOVERY

Discover your wobble! The numbers on the grid below increase in all directions from zero/zero at the center. Add the numbers left and right as well as up and down.

Enlarge or shrink the grid on a copier so the size is exact for the distance at which you will shoot. For example: At 25 yards, one MOA* is equal to a quarter (1/4th) inch.

Use this from various shooting positions. It tells you:

1. Your personal effective shooting distance Convert the measured wobble information to bullet flight error a <u>certain distance away</u>. 2. From which position you shoot best. 3. If horizontal deviation is worse than vertical. (Easy to identify and then correct.) 4. **BIG DEAL!** Enables you to dry fire and thus discover the same shooting errors that occur when you burn expensive ammunition.

*MOA = Minute of Angle. There are 60 MOA's in one degree.

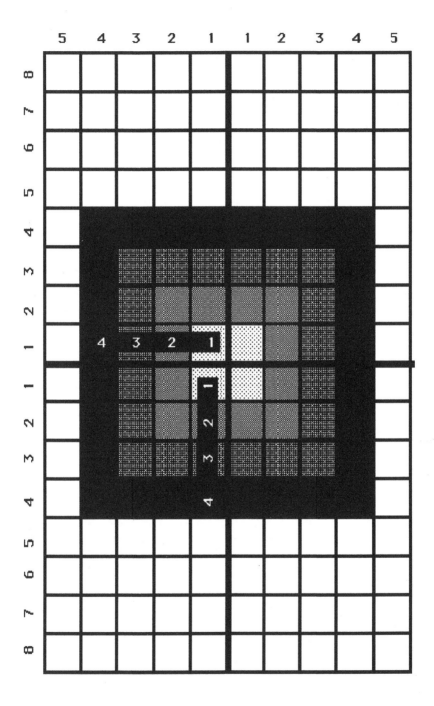

CONFLICTS INVOLVING FIREARMS

Handgun combat shooting requires a variety of skills. Learn them one at a time, then combine them to become a great combat handgunner. Each skill has specific definitions.

Presentation. This word defines the act of removing your handgun from its storage place and bringing it to bear on target. Start slowly; be deliberate. The real McCoy in combat will make you want to hurry. That's why some handgunners never walked on holy ground, but they have holey feet.

Probably the best is to draw your gun so that nobody sees it. For example, it remains in your purse, in a canvas tool bag, in a cut-out book, or under a newspaper. You're ready to shoot; watch your opponent's hands; if the trouble escalates, one trigger pull is all you need.

Marksmanship. No bullet will do any good for you unless it's well placed. We discovered wobble-measurement and how it defines your accuracy at a distance. What do you get from this information? Confidence, which is one of the critical elements needed for bullet placement under pressure.

You and your handgun can provide some *GREAT LIVIN' IN GRUBBY TIMES* (Survival book title by Path Finder). Surviving today requires a variety of survival implements plus skills to use them.

Two of them are handgun ownership and shooting proficiency.

Notice that we've developed a system that teaches you without your having to burn a lot of ammunition.

Bought a good handgun? It's useless if you can't make it place bullets when and where you need them. Added to that, you need to learn how to load it so the bullets you place are most effective.

In a later chapter, we'll show you the loading sequence so that your ammunition is super effective.

But you must develop this skill. Our wobble grid allows you to skip the range and ammunition cost it takes to learn accurate bullet placement.

Old advice for shooting rifle/pistol at long distance was "hold over," which means aim above your target. Holding over takes your target out of view. Not good, especially if your target moves. **Dave** has a much better system for shooting at targets far away: A dot on your front blade measures precise height as you raise it in the rear notch. Elevating your front blade makes your bullets reach out to a longer range with much better accuracy than you could possibly achieve by holding over a target.

TRIGGER FINGER POSTURE

You will never be a good shot unless your trigger finger acquires this one critical movement skill!

Never changing, straight-to-the-rear trigger squeeze. Reproduce what you see in this picture. Learn to feel it.

(Illustration taken from *SURVIVAL SHOTGUN.*)

ULTIMATE HANDGUNNER

CHAPTER 3
Night Firing

You need to be prepared for trouble anytime it may occur. Define trouble. It's criminal activity in which perpetrators (those who commit crime) act for personal gain. When does that most often occur? In darkness so they can't be observed very well and also to keep them from being identified.

Almost all of us practice with a handgun during daylight. Even if we practice on a range in the dark, the target area is lit.

This is a big reason (although one of many) that I urge homeowners to use a shotgun. You can easily miss with a handgun, even during the day. But a shotgun is sort of Biblical, it covers a multitude of sins. Inside a home, you gotta be the world's worst, trigger-jerking-pre-shot flinching gunner in order for you to shoot a miss.

One other reason I am so pro shotgun is shell design. You can ask most shotgunners to reload in a special way so that the projectiles will not go through walls and wound innocents.

But, back to handguns. Several sight arrangements can be purchased that will allow you to see your sights in the dark. For poor people, grip your gun so that the sights and barrel are in line with your forearm. When you do that, shots will land pretty much wherever your arm points.

(That's why grips that fit your hand so that your trigger finger comes around in the perfect squeeze positon are such a big deal. The first shot's recoil doesn't change what we call "your index," which is the way your hand holds your weapon in perfect position).

You go to a firing range, learn from an instructor how to shoot and practice. SITREP: You are a fairly competent shooter during the day. But then you hear a window break in your house during the night. You have handgun ready. Pitch black.

Following is a list of DO's and DO NOT's.

Do not,

1. Use a flashlight on your handgun because it discloses your location.

2. Speak or disclose your location with unnecessary noise.

3. Remember that muzzle flash reveals your location.

4. Speak to police without attorney present. Zip it!

Do:

Have a plan established for you and family. Got a safe room? Go there. (See *CONQUER CRIME*.)

Use gun sights you can see in the dark.

Chamber a round. Safety off. Trigger finger flat on the side of handgun in case you fall or are unsure of target.

Install motion switches that turn on house lights when someone passes by.

Call for help. Recommend you have cell phone plugged in and "9-1" dialed so that you have only to dial a "1" to complete the call.

Low voice on phone to police. Describe self so you are not mistaken for perp.

YOU VERSUS THE INTRUDER

It's a sorry fact of life that shooting a burglar might start a race war. Recent riots in Missouri and Illinois go to prove that the black community is on edge. My indicator? Price of Real Estate in Ferguson, MO. decreased severely. Trial of police officers in Freddie Gray case failed to convict.

Speeches by Al Sharpton have probably incited riots, along with destruction of property and personal injuries. All of the above plus other white vs black incidents have created police attitudes. Got a call from a resident complaining of someone in her house? Don't break the speed limit on the way. Avoid confrontation. Do not shoot the burglar.

Therefore; do the best you can to avoid shooting. See the master bedroom barricade in *Conquer Crime*. Recommended: Use intercom system in house to warn burglar, tell him to take whatever and get out. Peace.

BUT IT MAY NOT GO THAT WAY...

So much of our population has yielded to the temptation to try drugs. Marijuana is prevalent, legal in some parts of the US, and rightfully called an introductory drug. Death rate from overdose is severe. Therefore, this might happen. Drug influence compels the burglar to take it to the max. SITREP: Absolute darkness. You without shotgun. No potential hostage problem.

See *WAY BEYOND LOVE*, working title for my new fiction. Hero Jon teaches himself to use more than sight, i.e. hearing and scent recognition. You need to do the same.

Most druggies emit a foul odor and you may be able to detect where it's coming from. Don't shoot; wait. Hearing may help you. Got something you can toss away from you silently. Anything glass is a good idea because tossing it away from you may cause it to break and draw fire from your intruder. The combat rule applies: He who shoots first and doesn't hit will soon be shot at. Therefore, do not take any risks. The outcome of the situation is good if you don't get hurt. Wait it out. Sooner or later, police will arrive and handle the situation.

Crime has increased. If you bought a handgun and learned to use it, you'll be safer. Popular with some gun owners now: Sign says NRA Member or home protected by Mr. Smith and Mr. Wesson. Signs like these invite home burglaries because guns are popular in the underworld.

As the country goes downhill, the need for personal protection will increase. Use your senses to detect trouble. Use your common sense to wait it out or deal with it.

Don's new fiction features a 21-year-old super woodsman in Oregon who shoots a .22 magnum rimfire.

Why? No fear of running short on ammunition. He can carry 100 rounds into the woods easily. Of course, lightweight bullets are moved off their intended bullet flight path by crosswinds. So to make a critical shot, hero Jon has to maneuver so that winds are in line with bullet flight.

You can do the same with this trick (I invented) used by my fictional hero. He hung a two inch piece of yarn below the barrel AND installed a compass in the comb of his stock.

He pointed the rifle into the wind until the yarn blew parralel with the barrel. He noted the barrel direction twice.

1. Into the wind and
2. towards the target

The difference in degrees tells you what value to allow for windage.

For examples, 90° crosswind, **full** value of the sidewind for the distance of the shot. 45° would produce a vector about **half of full** value.

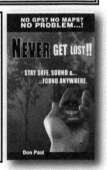

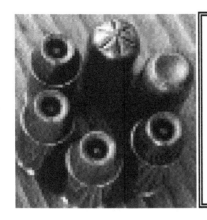

Mixing bullets in a revolver gives you versatility. Shot shell assures short range, sure hit and others offer long-range smack-ability.

Loaded this way, your handgun can perform a variety of chores and solve problems that are untouchable if you load with only one kind of bullet.

ULTIMATE HANDGUNNER

CHAPTER 4
Mix 'n Match

LOADING WITH EXOTIC BULLETS IN SEQUENCE

If you could inspect all of the handguns in the world, you would find that over 90% are loaded with only one kind of bullet. You can do a lot better.

I first advocated mix 'n match in my book, **CONQUER CRIME,** *How To Be Your Own Bodyguard.* The problem we solved at that time was penetrating some barriers and avoiding shotshell travel beyond what was needed. (We loaded shotshells wilth chopped up paper clips to keep them from going through house walls.) To **mix,** you will simply load with an assortment of bullets. Do that, and your handgun can do a variety of different chores.

Some will spread shot to insure at least some kind of impact. Much like the claw-punch to the face in Karate, it slows down the opponent, shocks him, and therefore provides extra time for any defensive shooter. Other bullets, such as Hydra-shocks and Hollow Points will spread out to create a large cavity after entering a target. Additional rounds will speed because they have more powder behind a lighter bullet. Still others (extra hard projectiles) will penetrate barricades like car doors and thick wood fences.

As far as handgun utility is concerned, we've always asked, "Why own a one-trick pony?" After all, it's simple to load your handgun so it performs a variety of tasks.

MIX 'N MATCH

Mix means load your handgun with a different kinds of cartridges for various tasks. Some will spread shot to insure impact. Other bullets, such as Hydra-shocks and Hollow Points will spread out to create a large cavity after entering a target. Additional rounds will speed because they have more powder behind a lighter bullet. Still others (extra hard projectiles) will penetrate barricades like car doors and thick wood fences. Dave cast a bullet that penetrated an engine block.

Match means all loads, in magzines or speed loaders, will be in the same sequence. Load every magazine and speed loader the same way. If you shoot a revolver, mark both your cylinder and your speed loader the same way. When you match up the marks, you always know the sequence in which the various rounds appear.

If you buy ammo, make sure to obtain some custom rounds. Perhaps trade half of your new box for half of a friend's so you each have a variety. Of course, test fire various cartridges.

You never know when, where or how a gunfight might occur. If you could predict, you could avoid the fight. However, with only a handgun for defense, what ammunition would you like to carry?

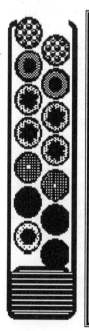

On top: Loads of #12 shot are LIFO, Last In, First Out. They insure some kind of hit. Hollow points follow, but by the time the first two rounds are gone, the shooter has the offensive advantage, and time to aim.

The next four rounds are hydra-shock rounds that make criminal shooting activity come to a sudden halt. After those, lead-antimony cast bullets provide super penetration.

Finally, we show three solid cast bullets with antimony added to the lead; therefore, they penetrate through most barriers, such as vehicle doors.

Note this: If round nosed, they ricochet like a flat rock on water. That's why so many lawsuits against LAPD are pending in Los Angeles. The body of LAPD officers voted for a different, non-ricocheting round. But the chief voted to keep them. Do you think that made the Trial Lawers Association happy?

SOME COMBAT SITUATION PROBABILITIES

Shot rounds out first ensure some kind of hit and therefore create shock in a perpetrator. That's especially true if you are in an enclosed area in the dark. An insured hit followed by a better bullet will put a sudden end to all conflict. If the perp is dressed in heavy clothing; (cold weather and he wears heavy wool overcoat, perhaps with wads of newspaper underneath) you need an armor piercing bullet. The same kind of penetration is also desirable if you're shooting against a perp behind a barricade or in an old domestic car.

Will your first shot most likely take place at close distance? That could happen. Often, you'll be surprised. That's the reason a shot shell is frequently loaded so it's the first to fire.

FOR THE HANDGUN HUNTER

Once again, mix 'n match. One main function for the handgunner is protection against snakes. So shot loads are in order. The same loads often provide lunch. Far up in the hills once, I ran low on food when I discovered a pond full of frogs. On another occasion, I brought down fat grouse.

While a discussion of ballistics is interesting, the practical question is this: Can you hold steady enough to reduce your cone of fire to be effective at long distance? How's your trigger finger? Straight to the rear?

MEMORIZING YOUR LOADING SEQUENCE

Once you determine a loading sequence for your handgun, load every magazine and speed loader the same way. If you shoot a revolver, mark both your cylinder (so you can feel it in the dark) and your speed loader the same way. When you match up the marks, you always know the sequence in which the various rounds appear.

The **only way** to solve a variety of problems in the field is to load with a variety of cartridges, each of which will do a specific chore. Will your first shot most likely take place at close distance? It can happen; most often, you'll surprised. That's one reason a shot shell is first up. Moreover, several of those chores can be life savers (like yours).

A much higher percentage of criminal encounters occur at night. Bad guys sleep most of the day (drugs) and gain psychological advantage when committing crime at night (they feel hidden and safe from being identified). This means that your own defensive gun activity may often occur in the dark. So, with revolvers, you have to be able to feel, rather than look at, what you are doing.

Placing the correect ammo in the correct sequence is a vital, life saving skill. Who's life? Yours!

What is most important for the hunter to know is this. Mix 'n match loading gives you utility in the field. I encountered a rattlesnake once and emptied a clip before I finally hit it with my .45 auto. A load of #8 shot would have saved me a lot of anxiety. Missing a vital area on a bear's head with a light load was foolish when I am pretty sure a heavy bullet to the body would have ended the dangerous fight that followed.

If you mix 'n match, then load your handgun with a variety of rounds, it's the same as if you carried three different handguns into the field. To any wilderness outdoorsman, that's the same as feasting or going hungry.

MEANWHILE, BACK ON THE STREETS

Once you have decided on your sequential cartridge pattern, stack your magazines (automatics) or load your cylinders. As mentioned–load all magazines and speed loaders the SAME WAY.

KNOWING WHERE YOUR BULLETS LAND

Unfortunately, you never know at what distance you might encounter an opposing force. Solve the bullet strike problem by sighting in for your most-encountered engagement distance. Vary your shooting distance when you practice. Let the gold bead or tritium dot on your front blade guide you into lining up your sights to compensate for the change in bullet strike.

HELPING YOU CHOOSE

Of course, wadcutters are poor choices for long range; wind resistance slows them down. How can you be sure? Go to a range. You need to test fire every kind of bullet you will carry.

Rest your weapon and fire carefully. Get perfect sight alignment and squeeze that trigger with the greatest care. Note where the bullet strikes. Perhaps you'll have to raise your blade in the notch to compensate for bullet drop. When you finish, you know exactly what your long distance zero or hold will be.

Of course, mix 'n match beats firing only one kind of bullet. It's the answer to almost all possible problems you'll encounter in the field.

When you know how each round performs, you and your handgun can handle any shooting situation with ability others can only dream about—especially all the wild criminals who operate at night in the streets.

Rest your weapon and fire carefully. Get perfect sight alignment and squeeze that trigger with the greatest care. Note where the bullet strikes. Perhaps you'll have to raise your blade in the notch to compensate for bullet drop. When you finish, you know exactly what your long distance zero or hold will be.

Of course, mix 'n match beats firing only one kind of bullet. It's the answer to almost all possible problems you'll encounter in the field.

When you know how each round performs, you and your handgun can handle any shooting situation with ability others can only dream about—especially all the wild criminals who operate at night in the streets.

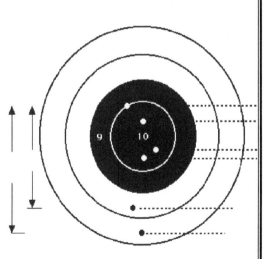

Dave shot this bullseye in order to accurately measure different bullet strikes at 25 yards. We scaled his target and copied it precisely on a computer.

It's interesting to note that heavier weight bullets strike higher. Why? More muzzle flip. The longest distance between bullet holes is 6.5". Note this. The different bullet strikes are up and down, which guarantees a hit on a vertical target.

21

My dad, police inspector B. B. Smith, told me this: Two armed robbers were trying to outrun a two -man Highway Patrol Car. Both passengers made it a running gun battle. Our cop was a good shot with his .38 Special revolver loaded with a mix—158 grain and 110 grain zinc Highway Masters—all of which he let fly.

The getaway driver failed to make a safe turn and struck a concrete bridge abutment at high speed. Bad driving? Nope.

Though the officer had aimed for the gas tank, his heavier zincs went low, ricocheted up off the highway under the car and had entered the driver's heel and buttocks. (Thus making it difficult to brake.) *Dave*

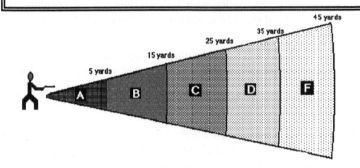

Shooter demonstrates bullet strike spread at increasing distances. This is why practice at short ranges helps. You, (the shooter), can analyze the spread of individual bullet shots and determine the cause. As we all know bullets landing in lower left of a target indicate trigger jerks. Other causes: Poor sight alignment because the shooter's eye focuses on the target rather than the front sight. Rounds landing high because of too much heel pressure on the pistol's stock.

You need to correct shooting errors and deficiencies so that your shot groups shrink. Why? That's the key to being able to hit from long distance. Being far away from your target promotes security, because the fecal part of our society can't shoot that well. You shoot accurately from a relatively safe distance against a criminal who sprays bullets and therefore has much **less** chance of hitting you.

Look at some of the defense loads you can use in a .38 Special. From left to right: Winchester 150 grain (Grn) bullet, 200 Grn bullet, Norma 158 Grn JSW (Jacketed Semi-wadcutter) Super Vel's 110 Grn SP, Winchester 110 Grn JHP (Jacketed Hollow Point). Last three are all Remington's 95 Grn, 125 Grn, and 158 Grn, all JHP's (Jacketed Hollow Points).

Photo from files of Dave Smith, retired California Highway Patrol.

ULTIMATE HANDGUNNER

CHAPTER 5
Lady Guns:
Modern Guns for Women

Frequently, both men and women buy too much gun. Way too much. I've done hundreds of call-in media shows on my book, **CONQUER CRIME,** and many have called to discuss the .44 mangl'ems they keep for home protection.

Of course, if you practice, many multiple hits will be easy to place. Israeli hit teams–well trained and highly professional–carry a light caliber because the noise is easy to suppress (silence). In addition to that, small gun–they prefer light weight and easy concealment. Try .22 magnum.

MOST IMPORTANT CHOICE: CALIBER

How big are you? Strong women may handle a .357 magnum. Can you carry the weight of a heavy gun with you <u>conveniently</u>? If not, you may get into the bad habit of leaving your fire power at home. Think: Will the gun you intend to buy fit in your purse?

In her book, *ARMED AND FEMALE,* Paxton Quigley lists various weapons by intimidation factor. She did it so well that we leave it out. Paxton is frequently employed by the major gun companies because she has so much experience on the gun ranges with women.

If you carry a short-barreled .22 mag, the noise from the first round you fire will shake up anybody. That's intimidation by sound. Finally, though, think of the best intimidation possible, by feel. With a .38 Special shooting hollow-cupped wadcutters, the sight, the noise and the wallop will solve all problems.

What can you afford? In a downturn economy, you may have to budget, not only for the gun, but for the ammo. Therefore, one good choice of caliber is .22, either in long rifle (not so powerful), or, better, the same .22 caliber in magnum. Hollow-point bullets are the best. Read the fiction section of *NEVER GET LOST* (128 pp. $8.88) and you will experience my hero's clever use of a 22. magnum lever action rifle. He overcomes the limitations of the caliber by maneuvering so that side winds were not a factor in shooting on a moonless night. For me, the .22 mag choice for both one of my handguns and a rifle was a good idea. Of course, I hunted with both. Here, the concern is self defense in a society slowly sinking into uncontrollable criminal activity.

If the wobble grid tells you long range shots will miss, why buy a .357 mangl'em that will shoot a far distance? Also, consider this: Wobble always increases during high stress. What else might cause wobble to increase? Handgun weight. Heavy handguns cause more wobble because of muscle fatigue. Additionally—big gun recoil and noise often create trigger jerk which makes accurate shooting impossible.

You are not allowed to miss! No matter what the cause, sight misalignment or wobble, any deviation more than 16 minutes means you shouldn't take a shot farther away than 50 yards. If that be the case, why buy a big caliber with a long barrel? ALL YOU REQUIRE IS A SMALL CALIBER / SHORT BARREL TO DELIVER ENOUGH FIREPOWER WITHIN THE DISTANCE AT WHICH YOU CAN HIT.

So the absolute rule for women who buy guns is: Don't buy a gun that shoots beyond the effective distance at which you can hit. "Effective" means with penetration and expansion. When a woman owns a gun she can shoot effectively ONLY AT SHORT RANGE, she gets several benefits. 1. Light weight. 2. Concealability. 3. Confidence. 4. Undisturbed bullet placement.

Remember from the accuracy chapter—what we're after is **operational accuracy**. The gun, itself, may be super accurate. Custom-made ammo may be precision stuff. You may even be a decently-trained shooter. But you may not be able to shoot this particular weapon. You have to assess your abilities carefully before you buy too much gun. If you do buy too much gun, you have a remedy: Download for it. The .357 accepts .38 Specials.

GRIPS

In her book, *ARMED AND FEMALE*, Ms. Quigley writes, "The next and perhaps most important after-market customizing that must be done to almost every revolver, and especially to a woman's gun, is the installation of the proper-size grips." To which I add: Absolutely. If you don't make the grip fit your hand, you won't be able to hold on after firing just once.

Women who buy guns may be told that long range is a factor. As a matter of fact, that's how they practice (25 feet). Think about this, however. You most likely won't use this handgun for hunting. No need for a long-distance shot, so there's no need for a long barrel with fancy sights. Women's weapons are for protection when a criminal attacker is nearby.[*] That's why any automatic handgun for a lady is not a good idea.

For a first-time gun buyer, we recommend revolvers. They're reliable. Autos are complex and require expertise, which means plenty of practice. Consider this also; Ladies with long fingernails have a hard time shoving shells into an automatic's magazine.

Furthermore, a revolver shoots from inside a purse without the automatic slide action snagging on other contents in the handbag.

[*]See: *CONQUER CRIME, How To Be Your Own Bodyguard*, $12.95 from *www.survival-books.com.*

BARREL LENGTH

Short barrels are more compact, easier to carry, and of course, harder to grab (See *CONQUER CRIME*, in which we explain that many criminals would rather die than let themselves be conquered by a woman). Therefore, they'll grab.

Even though a sight alignment error with a short barrel is worse than the same error with a longer barrel, who cares when the shooting distance is short?

SIGHT SYSTEMS

Laser sights can be extremely helpful when training because you can see the dot move on our wobble grid—either as a result of excessive wobble or jerky trigger snaps.

For ladies' combat shooting, we don't recommend anything that relies on battery power. Unless you check your batteries, you could rely on sights that won't power up. Also, lasers add bulk to your weapon. Dot telescopes are also bulky. Worse, they require time in which to locate a target. So the standard, old, notch-and-blade sight is our favorite. However, the way they come from the factory, they need improvement.

It may be that you will aim this handgun. Stare at the spaces between the blade and the notch on both sides. For real-life shooting, you need to stare at the front sight and make sure you have an even distance on both sides of the blade. Perhaps ask a gunsmith to widen the notch in the rear sight. That will cut down on your target acquisition time.

A small, luminous dot on the front and rear of your barrel enables you to see your gun at night so you can shoot from the hip with reliable accuracy.

If your sights don't have dots buy cheap illumination ("SCRIBBLES" from Ben Franklin's Stores), or any luminous sighting system Otherwise, your handgun is only operational during daylight. **Not good!** Most crime occurs at night.

In these tough times, more women need to carry a handgun. When you know you can hit from a certain distance, choose the caliber and bullet that will perform two tasks:

1. **NOT SMACK** the shooter's hands so hard that they fear the pain of recoil. Other factors can be ignored, but do not buy a gun that punishes you when you shoot it.

2. Provide enough power to subdue an intruder. You need enough kinetic energy to make the round penetrate **and** open up inside your target's body. Look in the tables found in most gun manuals to find that caliber. Then, keep on practicing. When you carry a gun you can shoot, you'll exude confidence. That's an attitude street thugs will read like a book. Thus, you'll be safe.

ULTIMATE HANDGUNNER

CHAPTER 6
Incoming:
The Art and Science of Getting Shot At!

Dave and I believe it's a rip-off tragedy if we don't teach you this. In all of the violent movies and TV shows we see, the good guy prevails. Even if he gets shot, it's "just a scratch." Of course, we all identify with the shooter—the good guy who wins and rides off with the Hollywood honey.

Further aggravation arises because of the print media's focus on shooting. Draw your handgun this way; sight on that; blast the bad guys. You'll see pictures of all kinds of shooters winning the gun battles.

WHAT YOU WON'T SEE BUT MUST CONSIDER

If you draw your handgun, chances are more than decent someone else will have a similar gun pointed at you. In fact, politicians have created some terrible rules of engagement. You have to wait until you feel your life is threatened before you can respond, and you can't respond with any more force than that which was facing you. Therefore, you can't go around with your gun drawn.

That's why the unconventional presentation is such a good idea. You need to have your hand on your weapon while it's concealed in your purse or jacket or pocket or backpack or perhaps under a towel. You need to be ready to shoot if the bad guy starts to draw, doesn't heed your warning or moves closer with obvious intent. Later you either remove your hand from the gun (still concealed) or you shoot as soon as you find out that the threat you suspected becomes a reality.

27

Now follow this line of thought: You can't use more force than someone uses on you. You can only shoot when you are faced with the threat of losing life. If you do draw your handgun, the other guy certainly has a right to fear for his life, so you've just elevated a conflict to a lethal level. Therefore, isn't it logical to believe... Any time you resort to handgun force, it's highly probable someone will shoot at you?

Knowing this, why is it that nobody has instructed you on how to get shot? Granted, it ain't fun to read and think about. But learning how to shoot the other guy is only half what you need to know. If we don't give you some advice on this vital subject, we don't do our jobs as writers. Thus we get to: "Incoming 101, The Art and Science of Getting Shot At." Here's the course synopsis: DON'T!

Simply telling you "don't get shot" may not work. Since the ACLU has gone to court and relieved the overcrowding in prisons, society now is overcrowded with criminals. Every state in the union now contains tens of thousands of these germs running loose in society. Where does someone go when let out of prison? Back to the gang because his friends and acquaintances are there.

So chances are good that you will be shot at. First, let's think about skipping the event. Since bad guys can't hit what they can't see, hiding is a good idea. If possible, let's dive behind a barricade. Once safe, you can solve this gunfight problem.

You need to understand the difference between cover and concealment. A bullet stopping barricade provides cover. This is the definition of concealment: Anything through which the other guy's bullet might travel, even though it hides you. Wood fences and some trees, and house walls, for example, are not cover. Anything that hides you but can easily be penetrated by a bullet can only be considered as concealment. Cover might be a big oak tree or a concrete brick wall.

Here's a life-saving rule: If you're only concealed during a fire fight, shoot and move. Moving is absolutely necessary because the opposition will shoot at your muzzle flash or the sound of gunfire. Stay concealed, but be looking for bullet-stopping cover. Likewise, check to see if you can't penetrate what your opponent believes to be cover. (That's why mix 'n match loading is so important. It broadens the usability of your handgun. More than that, it may keep you alive because you carry a cartridge that can solve a serious problem.)

How does one shoot? Sight. He sees you, then he aims and pulls the trigger. How else might he sense your presence? Sound. It's a relative thing. When you either make more noise than he or camp next to a noisemaker (running water over rocks) while he's slightly less noisy, you can't hear him. That's why you shouldn't use earphones for entertainment in a high-burglary area. You can't hear a door hinge squeak. Is there another way? Smell. We don't use that in the city too much, but in the woods we pick up campfire scents, cigarette smoke (I've smelled it a mile away) and perhaps human odor.

So now you enter into conflict. Success or failure depends on his and your **human senses**. Knowing that, how could you win? Here it is:

That was my function in Special Forces. We fooled the enemy when we all looked like bushes. Camouflage kept him from seeing us. He couldn't hear us because we taped our dog tags, oiled our boots, and stayed away from naturally noisy places such as moving water. We also were very careful in terrain that might bounce sound. We buried all of our body wastes–both kinds. To summarize: Nobody could see us, hear us, or smell us– we took away the enemy's senses.

Let's apply the principle to you. First, don't wear bright clothes at night. As anybody knows, certain fabrics reflect light to a greater degree than others. In law enforcement, the policy might call for white shirts and ties. Therefore, wear a dye-darkened undershirt and immediately remove the white shirt and any ornaments as soon as combat begins.

Second, let the other guy work in the light. Stay in the shadows as much as possible. Don't move. Wait for him to move. Hiding in shadows provides a good advantage, especially if you can move undetected from one shadow to another. A difference between the light intensity in which he's positioned and your own darkness will often enable you to win. Light up the outside yards in your home. You can buy lights with sensor switches that turn on and flood the area like a stage when anyone walks under them.

Keep your eyes night-operational! If you use a campfire at night, wear an eye patch over your gun-sighting eye. It takes a long time before your eye's iris expands so you can see in the dark, but it only takes a quick second to make it close down. If you've been staring into a campfire with both eyes, any idiot can deal with you from a distance away and you won't be able to see him. Also, don't stare into city light sources at night. Especially with headlights shining in your direction, close at least your gun sighting eye so you maintain your night vision.

What about sound? How could you enhance theirs and make yours minimal? In your own city area, you set the ground so that anything moving makes noise. Gravel pits outside your windows go "crunch" the minute someone steps there. Inside a building, take off your shoes so you make no sound. Incidentally, test any hunting boots you buy. Duplicate the hearing of a deer by using a microphone hanging near your boots while you walk in them. Turn up the volume so you can hear what a deer will hear when you wear them in the woods.

Want to improve your sense of both smell and hearing? Get a dog. Dogs can smell a stranger. I often used my dog as a pillow in the woods. I covered her with a space blanket to keep her warm; she stayed on guard. On several occasions, she growled lightly to wake me up because of a bear or coyote upwind. I had my .41 mag ready long before anything came close to camp.

Stay upwind and trust your nose. You really will be able to smell a guy who is sweating because gunfighting makes everybody nervous. It also creates gastric disturbance. Your enemy may produce gaseous scent signals that lead right to him.

Now, let's make the other guy easier to see. You need to sense him better than he can sense you to create a battle advantage. When all is said and done, if they can't see, hear or smell you, but you can detect them, you'll be safe.

TO AVOID DETECTION

You have choices, a couple of which are: Shoot first and best, or dive for cover. Cover is the best choice because it keeps you safe. Shooting is risky for two reasons: A. You disclose your location and expose part of your body. B. You may hit—only to be sued afterwards. So a quick move to cover is best.

> Diminish or take away his senses while strengthening yours.

However, what if cover isn't available? As your drill sergeant, I gotta first ask, "Why weren't you operating near cover?" You don't have to run down the middle of a street. Near buildings you can always jump into a doorway or hide behind a parked car, etc. This is the way I want you to be: Outstanding in your field. That's one word; not two. Don't be out, standing in your field. Nevertheless, what if someone tries to shoot you while you're in the middle of nowhere?

Don't forget the theory of relative target size. Shrink your body. Then shoot a lot. Given equal shooting ability and equal firepower, you double your chances of hitting first if you simply reduce your target size.

To make your defense complete, consider what you might do if you can't get to either concealment or cover, and you don't want to shrink your body. Wear protection. A variety of body armor is available which will keep almost all handgun slugs from penetrating your body. Even a thick book taped to a shirt over your heart could save your life.

Contrary to what you see in the movies, you can take a hit and live. Many people think handgun wounds are fatal, but lots of people who were shot are still alive and well today.

UNNECESSARY HANDGUN DEATHS

People die after being shot by handgun for one of two reasons. A. The bullet destroys their body physiologically. Most often that's a CNS (Central Nervous System) hit. B. They kill themselves psychologically. "A" doesn't happen very often. "B" happens a lot. If you're alive and bleeding, you didn't die—and you won't—as long as you remain calm and get some decent medical attention. The single exception is a CNS hit, in which event, you won't feel it anyway. Don't let your brain send you to judgement before your time.

DEVELOP AN UNBEATABLE ATTITUDE

Become invincible. It's a state of mind as well as body. Special Forces people often develop a life-preserving attitude. The training is such a bear that people who survive it really believe nothing can kill them. You don't have to employ those methods of severe self training, although I recommend them. If you can, keep your body in top shape and your mind clear. Learn to shoot by rote with frequent practice. If you should get into a shoot out, you need to shoot back, move, seek cover, and try to count your shots so you know what kind of bullet is next up. Assess your situation.

As far as attitude goes, just remember this, <u>it ain't over</u>. You may be down and bleeding, but that's the best time to get tricky and settle the score. Never give up. If you are losing this confrontation, get mad and fight back! "The best defense is a good offense."

GUNFIGHT PRIORITIES—A CHECKLIST

A. Before it even starts. Plan. You know your areas of operation. Think, "what will I do if . . ."

B. Eliminate the possibility of getting hit. Take cover. Destroy your enemy's ability to deliver fire. Often, you do both at the same time. A round with good penetrating ability can make all the difference.

C Use concealment when cover is inadequate, but don't stay in one place. If you don't score, count on return fire. The first time you shoot, you advertise your hiding place.

D Engage only if necessary. When should you engage? Only when you know you can neutralize the threat without risk to your own person. Never let anger or fear be the basis of any decision. Those two emotions cause soldiers to charge machine gun nests with pistols—and win medals—posthumously.

E. If you possibly can, identify his weaponry as soon as it starts. Stay where you are. When you know you can hit at the enemy's range, then, maybe <u>engagement</u> will be a relatively safe thing to do. Find out for sure in the next chapter.

Stands out
like a fruit at
an NRA meeting.

Adversary

Almost
invisible,
soundless.

You

The most fundamental concept of tactics goes like this: You analyze the enemy's capability. You learn during practice and training exactly what you can do. Then you match what you can do against what he can't.

WHY SHOOTING VICTIMS WENT TO A HOSPITAL

They . . .

1. were "situation blind." They didn't pay attention to the people around them or what was going on.

2. thought crime would never happen to them.

3. never considered themselves as possible victims.

4. believed that everyone is a good person. (Freud's idea, not the Bible's).

5. never owned, carried or used an offensive weapon, such as a gun, knife, walking stick or club.

6. believed police signs, "to protect and serve."

With no help around, at least shrink your body size as you shoot. The smaller target you present, the less likelihood of your being hit. Nobody likes to think of getting shot AT, but failure to consider the possibility will cause lack of knowledge and zero preparation.

You can save a handgunner's life—your own.

To do that, you need to:

1. Know what to do and practice until you don't have to think about it.

2. Be mentally prepared to act.

YOU MAY HAVE TO SLEEP IN THE WOODS...

...when it's dangerous. Use your hammocks.* Sleep half sitting up in one hammock that is tied to a tree. Then cover yourself with another hammock on which you tie leaves for camouflage. Rain? Cover up with a garbage bag. Bird seed on the ground near you will cause you to wake up in the morning if any person or animal approaches. (Birds will flutter when they fly away.)

*Get a free copy: *24 Ways to use Your Hammock* from
www.survival-books.com

33

Landmark book on new, outdoor knife uses. Outdoor Life Book Club selection. *American Survival Magazine* said, "...16 of the most innovative and informative chapters on knives and knife uses ever written." Just under 40,000 sold. 136 pp.

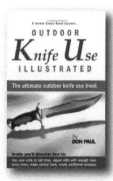

A former Green Beret teaches...

OUTDOOR

Knife Use

ILLUSTRATED

The ultimate outdoor knife use book

by
DON PAUL

San Francisco Shoot Out

Over 100 rounds were fired. Whacko wants to play "The news will make you famous." He decides to make an impression on the world through sensational media. Dead: Suspect and one officer. Wounded: One officer and one citizen.

Dead officer was shot while trying to reload a revolver. The wounded officer was barricaded behind a house wall. Suspect merely used a rifle (probably with FMJ ammo) and shot through the wall to wound the officer.

Although the suspect was shot with Treasury load .38 Special, his bullet proof vest stopped the slug. Finally, a police sniper with a rifle had enough power to penetrate the vest.

ILLEGAL GUNS FOR RENT

Those who want to commit crimes without the weapon involved being traceable, can rent them. Felons, especially who can't buy a gun from a dealer, rent from an underground broker. The gun isn't traceable to the broker, either, because it was stolen and the broker fenced it, probably from a drug dealer who paid for it with drugs. This is common knowledge.

But if politicians declare all guns illegal because the United States made a treaty with a foreign country, I am sure all the rental gun brokers in the country will turn theirs in. Yeah, right...

Most senators and of course, Obama of "Fast & Furious" fame, lobby hard for the Brady Bill. One senator shouted, "A pox on anyone who calls this weapon a sporting firearm." Comedian Dave Letterman had a better idea: A gun-type law that says you have to wait five days before buying a politician.

Not many single-action, fast draw artists have stood on holy ground, but more than a few have holey feet:)

ULTIMATE HANDGUNNER

CHAPTER 7
Modern Handguns

In *GREAT LIVIN' IN GRUBBY TIMES*, you learned that pistols should be your last choice in survival weapons because they are difficult to shoot. It would appear that handgun bullet placement problems are solved if the sights are aligned on your target just before you shoot. But that doesn't happen.

Reason with me: If the bullet flew wild, then the barrel was aimed at the wild location which the bullet struck. But the barrel contols the bullet's flight. Sights control where the barrel is aimed. Why did the bullet fly wild when the sights were perfectly aligned? Many shooters who miss never find out why, The gun goes "boom," recoils, and leaves the shooter with practically no way to discover why there is no new hole in the target.

"But the sights were aligned when I shot," you say.

"Correct," I answer.

Conclusion: The shooter disturbed the sight alignment with bad finger discipline on the trigger.

In sort-of Biblical terms: **Many buy; few practice.**

Handguns are expensive, have limited range, and with few exceptions place third in the hierarchy of weapons. Why? They don't have the power of shotguns or rifles. But handguns are concealable; and require only one hand to shoot, and good power at short range. That's convenient.

Think of handguns for one of two uses: Hunting and defense. For hunting, you can go with a long-barreled revolver in a hip holster. I hunted black bear for years with a Ruger single action .357 magnum revolver. To get a better sight picture on a bullseye during practice, I adjusted my sights for a six o'clock hold. Bad mistake.

I held my sights high high center chest. But the round went in higher, of course. I thought I missed! He roared out of that tree, obviously intent on killing me after I caused his pain. Head down with claws in the tree bark, he moved quickly. I shot again at the center of his body, but jerked the trigger (Scared? Hurried? Who knows?) Immediately, there was a running bear-dog fight. Later on, the bear rolled over and died.

What's to learn from this? Zero your handgun so it places bullets right over the blade. Perhaps install a dot on your front sight so you can elevate the front blade to shoot accurately from a distance.

If you mix 'n match, you'll have special rounds in your speed loader. Some choices are: Jacketed hollow points for maximum wound cavity, shot loads for snakes or birds, a duplex load for close distance, and a penetrator to go through a barricade. My co-author, CHP Rangemaster Dave Smith cast some bullets that ventilated an engine block.

Practice in the dark; load by feel only. Learn to reload revolvers, clear jammed automatics, release safeties, etc. without looking. Ask your local gunsmith to make dummie rounds without primer or powder. Practice! In my book, *CONQUER CRIME, How to Be your Own Bodyguard*, you'll learn that most crime occurs after dark. That's the best time to train and become confident.

"Revolvers really are best — but only for the first six rounds." *Dave*

AUTOMATICS ARE POPULAR

We see an increasing number of automatics on the streets. When we say auto to describe pistols, we mean autoloader. Autos hold more than revolvers do. They also reload easily.

For automatics, you stuff a full magazine into the magazine well from underneath. When you empty the magazine that is in the handgun's well, you push **one** button to let that empty one drop out. The slide stays to the rear. Then you jam a new loaded magazine into the well, thumb the slide release (slide rams forward to place a new round into the chamber). Example: *LETHAL WEAPON I* in which actor Mel Gibson shot two full magazines at a helicopter.

Autos require maintenance and that maintenance is critical. If you don't clean and lubricate them, they have a nasty habit of "failing to feed." which means not smoothly ejecting an empty casing and loading another live round. The result is the worst noise you'll ever hear in a gunfight: "click."

For most shooters, the big magnums are a poor choice. After 20 rounds from one of the big magnum pistols, I start loosing trigger control. Powerful pistols are big, heavy, and cumbersome. Ask yourself: Would I rather have a small weapon with me often, or keep a heavy, combat hog at home?

Never buy more handgun than you can shoot with comfort and accuracy. Hitting with a .22 round is far better than a miss from a .44 Magnum. Just fire more shots.

Opinions on caliber vary. Although .25 and .32 ACP autos are in common use, they just don't have the smack for defense. We leave out the .41 and .44 magnum calibers. They pack too much smack to be shot accurately by average people. Dave's dad calls them "44 mangl-ems."

For the revolver purchaser who won't be practicing much, single actions have some advantages. Think of safety; if you don't deliberately cock the weapon, it won't fire. Single actions are smaller and lighter, even though they chamber a powerful round. You only have to learn one kind of trigger pull. Because of longer barrels and the single action (light) trigger pull, these guns shoot more accurately, even from the hip. *Dave*

In between small and large, you'll find several to choose from. Don recommends a .357 magnum because it shoots the .38 Special. When you are comfortable with the .38, you can graduate to magnum.

Don't disregard rimfire. Purchase a .22 magnum; buy 500 rounds which take up the space of a pint of milk. Some .22 revolvers come with an extra cylinder chambered for the .22 Winchester Magnum.

Longer sight bases found on long barrels provide more accuracy. In addition, long barrels produce improved bullet velocity. A six-inch barrel might shoot 100 fps faster than a four inch. (See CONQUER CRIME, How To Be Your Own Bodyguard.

Handguns lack power at long range, and require skill to shoot. Become totally familiar with yours. Dry fire it. Learn to load magazines in the dark. Think about many major cities (Detroit) in which a high percentage of street lights have been shot out. Why? When a cop stops someone wearing a hoodie and sunglasses, the cop is at a visual disadvantage. The last light that came into his eyes (headlights) closed down his iris.

The guy in the hoodie takes his sunglasses off and he can almost see in the dark.

Spend the time to learn exactly how to shoot the handgun of your choice. After you become a competent handgunner during day and at night, you will be your own bodyguard, and you can keep your house and family safe .

Too many "bells and whistles." A real "space gun." We named it that—not for the way it looks, but for the huge space it occupies.

Competition shooting has given rise to shooting methods that simply **will not work** in most real-life circumstances. Even with a good gun and special ammunition, many shooters simply can't hit a target during the pressure of combat. That's one good reason for shot loads.

ULTIMATE HANDGUNNER

CHAPTER 8
Handgun Use

Unlike rifles and shotguns handgun shooting requires a lot of skill. When Path Finder published *EVERYBODY'S OUTDOOR SURVIVAL GUIDE*, we hired Army Green Beret Silver Star winner and black belt judo expert Rick Woodcroft to write on several subjects. In his chapter on hand-to-hand combat, he quotes Confederate General Jubal Early, who said "Get there fustus with the mostest." Handgunners need to learn that.

TIMES HAVE CHANGED

Pistol shooting today dictates that you practice for combat. Crime in America is now horrific (See *CONQUER CRIME*). We lead the world in prison population.

Handguns are designed to be shot during the day; most criminal conflicts occur at night. You'll be amazed at the difference. During criminal enterprise both you and the felon face each other. A logical outcome of a lethal weapon is this: The loser goes to judgement and the winner goes to jail. Ask George Zimmerman, who shot and killed Trevon Martin in Feb 2012, in Florida, a "stand your ground" State. Florida's prosecutors (prudently* in my opinion) charged Zimmerman with a felony.

*Failing to charge him would have led to the supercharged rioting of the black community. Think back to L.A. and the Rodney King riots.

To determine the effectiveness of any handgun at long range, ask two questions: A. Can you shoot well enough to place a bullet on target that far out? B. Will the projectile have any stopping power after slowing down way out there?

OTHER FACTORS

Is your wobble small or do the sights on your handgun dance around? Does your trigger finger have a Ph.D. or does it wiggle like a kindergarten kid trying to pick his nose? How's your vision? Are your sights highly visible? See your gunsmith or darken your sights with candle fire. For night firing, install luminescent dots.

If you shoot at night and miss, you can count on the muzzle flash of your weapon giving away your position. You absolutely need to get behind cover (See: *GREAT LIVIN IN GRUBBY TIMES*. Paul. Ref. Difference between cover and concealment.)

SHOOTING FOR REAL

My own PAUL system: *Platform Accuracy, Unitized Level*. It locks up the weapon by pushing with the gun hand and pulling with the other. The shooter learns to fire from the hip with a level barrel because most handgun fights occur on level floors or streets.

CREATE STRESS DURING PRACTICE

Competition creates nervous stress. Leisurely practice will NOT prepare you for combat. Run up a hill in the dark before shooting so your heart's pumping (racing pulse) the way it will when full of adrenaline. You need that. Shoot at a target under the pressure of time while in competition with other shooters.

THEORY OF RELATIVE TARGET SIZE

Shooting a handgun from the standing position is most unstable. Worse than that, when standing, you expose your whole body. On one knee, you're half size. The average street gangster won't get a round off before you drop down, especially if you shoot while you move. Also, (pay attention here) most first shots are high anyway because it's common to hold the muzzle up when shooting from the hip. That's why banking a round or two off the ground is best.

There's more: Positions to reduce relative size provides the double benefit of steadying your weapon. You become hard to hit while increasing your chances of hitting. Kneeling with a two-handed hold while resting against a barricade will produce a steady, no-wobble shot. On our wobble grid, discover which position is easiest to get into. Even more important, answer this question: Which position causes the least amount of wobble?

When you shoot against an enemy, failure to hit means "incoming." "Miss" is what you need your opponent to do. Imagine yourself on a firing range in a shooting contest. From the firing line, other shooters fire at a 12" bullseye, but your bullseye is half that size. In combat shooting I want your opponent to have a disadvantage like that. Out in the open, reduce your body size to less than 50% so you double his chances of missing.

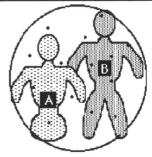

CONE OF FIRE---SIX FEET FROM HANDGUN WITH 24 INCH JERK / WOBBLE

A sits
B Kneels

41

SQUEEZE

Basic trigger control is a slow squeeze, a gentle, firm and slow pressure increase on the trigger straight to the rear. It takes a while to learn.

Always use the same spot on your finger, positioned in the same place on your trigger, and be careful to watch your sights as the hammer falls. If you can't do that while completely relaxed in your home, you certainly won't be able to while under stress.

After a slow squeeze, graduate. Increase pressure on the trigger more rapidly. Your finger should already know what it feels like to come straight to the rear. Do that now—only faster.

Bullet delivery follow-through. It ain't over 'till it's over. Many shooters makes this mistake under pressure. They align the sights, create a sight picture (on target) squeeze to the rear, and abandon the whole procedure just as the gun fires. This is best: Fire and "hold that thought" for a second after the gun goes off.

COVER

You need to look for cover in any situation that could be dangerous. Don't get over confident because you hide behind glass, a house wall, or a hollow core door. If the bullet looking for you came out of a .357 cartridge and is designed to penetrate, you'll even be at risk behind some solid trees.

Once behind cover, use a stationary object as a rest for your pistol. Practice that way. On a close-in target, you wouldn't bother with a rest, but the Lord has blessed you if you get into a hot lead exchange at a far distance and a tree is nearby. With a steadied weapon and almost all of your body protected, you'll increase your chances of survival many times over.

AVOID SHOOTING HIGH

You may shoot high or low. Low might not matter because of bullet-ricochet off a hard surface. But high is a common disaster. Many who fire from the hip are inclined to shoot high because looking at the tip of the handgun in relation to the target causes the shooter to elevate the muzzle.

The probability of losing your grip after one shot increases if the material in your grips is somewhat slippery. Palm sweat does that. Surfboard wax is a good remedy.

TARGET ACQUISITION

Get your sights on target. But at short distance, forget bringing your weapon up anywhere near your eyes; it takes too long. The sights on your handgun are for distances over 25 feet. In many cases, you aim at a target by sound. Why? Frequently at night, you can't see your target or your sights. The plan: Turn your head to listen to any noise so that your nose is pointing in the direction of what you hear. Next, turn your torso so it's in line with your head. Then, with a two handed, isosceles hold, point your handgun out in line with your nose and squeeze.

RELATIVE TARGET SIZE

A   B

In the movie *THE BODYGUARD*, Kevin Costner chases an assassin in the snow. He falls to his knees and closes his eyes. Why? On both knees, he reduced his personal target area by more than half. Then with eyes closed, he could concentrate on listening to the sound of crunching snow and shoot in that direction.

Here's how it all applies: You can shoot while you pop into a smaller stance. Once you get into that stance, you reduce your chances of taking an incoming round. How much? By the same percentage as your personal reduction in target size. Proof that "stand-up" is for comedy; not gun battle.

Practice this way. It will help you to shoot accurately in pitch blackness. One training exercise: In the wilderness, use doggie toys such as a rubber ball with noise makers. One person tosses, the other (blindfolded) shoots at the sound when the toy hits the ground.

Dave regards ammunition as a precious commodity and he doesn't care for ricochet rounds. Also, he wants your focus to be intent on hitting one small part of the target, nothing else. Once you've fired, keep on firing until you know for certain the threat has been eliminated—totally. Be ready to hammer more rounds home; it's never over until it's really over. *CONQUER CRIME, How To Be Your Own Bodyguard* recommends firing a final round in the air (legal reasons).

Sight picture on right is perfect and exactly what you need before the gun fires as a surprise. Two pictures on left, show wrong sight alignment caused by finger pressure to the side instead of a straight and strict to-the-rear trigger movement. Add a gold bead or white dot to your front blade for higher visibility at night. This is the time when most serious gun action occurs.

Automatic handguns provide you with plenty of fire power. With a high-capacity automatic, this is highly recommended: fire one or two so they ricochet off the surface between the two of you. Rounds on the ground ricochet upwards to make a nasty noise and perhaps a nastier wound. Much like a "ke-ai" in Karate, it de-stabilizes the enemy. Move and shoot because cover decreases your chances of being hit. Plus this: you often achieve bullet break up and the fragments can do real damage.

I taught a master Sgt in the Army how to do this and he used the technique in Iraq. Worked fine.

DEVELOP A SHOOTING PLAN

As you know, in range, power and accuracy, handguns finish third behind rifles and shotguns. However, most handgun confrontations are pistol vs. pistol so you need a shooting plan. Guaranteed, you won't create a shooting plan while you're being shot at. Develop your shooting plan now around these vital elements:

1. Remember: **Action beats reaction.** In practice, develop your presentation and target acquisition speed. (Draw! Shoot!) Either by direct fire or by bouncing a ricochet off the ground at your target, be first.

2. Range, the distance from you to the target. From your MOA wobble results you know the distance at which you can place an accurate round. Is he farther away than you can shoot accurately? Take cover; perhaps let a round go while _moving_.

3. How far you have to run in order to reach cover. If you can get one or two rounds off—enough to suppress incoming fire while you move—go for the cover. As soon as you're secure, you can either call for help or swap lead with relative safety. No cover? Get your body target small and steady your weapon.

4. Ammo to waste? How much do you carry? Consider your basic load. When Dave carries his gun, he always brings an extra mag. If I were working in law enforcement in a city, a stacked 9 mm magazine with two back-up mags would be more appropriate. That way, I can carry a better variety of ammunition and I can waste a tactical round or two. Some of my ammo sizzles and some bullets are hard enough to penetrate elephant skin. I carry enough ammo to provide fire suppression, disable vehicles, punch through barriers, etc. Reloading not only provides cheap practice, it also provides the variety of projectiles and velocity you may someday need.

5. Are you a solo act, or do you have a good co-defense shooting partner? My book GREAT LIVIN in GRUBBY TIMES explains how two good team members working together are much better than three untrained opponents. Never let both guns be empty at the same time. With a partner, practice shooting as a team.

In the movies, one guy yells, "Cover me." and takes off running. Don't do that! Several disasters could occur. The message didn't get through. The covering partner was on round 12 of a 15 round mag. His gun jams. He himself delivers the same message and moves, knowing that you will "cover" him.

6. Develop a plan for both night and day. Available light is an important element in developing a shooting plan. Furthermore, if you only have limited time for practice, do it at night. Learn muzzle flash, movement in the dark with only one good (non-shooting) eye, and shooting at noise. Modify your weapon so you can see the line-up of your sights and barrel in the dark (Scribbles–3-D Paint, about $5 in a small bottle, Ben Franklin stores).

No matter day or night, always try to position yourself so you are in less light than your enemy. Day or night, position so that the light source is behind you. For defense shooters—people who will be defending a home or acting as a security guard for others, put motion detector lights outside your house. Set night lights to shine on your intruder. You stay in the dark.

WHAT TO SHOOT AT?

Hit what's available. If you can see it, bless it by making it holey. As long as <u>you</u> are still and searching, the advantage is yours. Perhaps improve your view. Under cars you can see for a long distance while behind good cover. Drop down, level your barrel and put a round through your enemy's ankle.

You lose your ability to see a target in darkness when you come into a dark building from daylight with no proper night vision preparation.

In combat, the second after you shoot, move. MUZZLE FLASH does two things:

1. Causes you to lose your night vision.

2. Advertises your position.

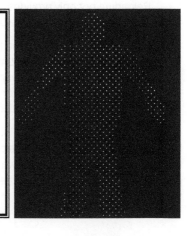

DRY FIRING TO LEARN TRIGGER CONTROL

You'll never be sure where your rounds will land if your trigger finger is uneducated. That's why this is such a critical element to learn in the shooting process. Without being able to squeeze to the rear every time, learning target acquisition (sighting) won't help much.

Therefore, you need to exercise your trigger finger until every round you fire never disturbs your sight alignment. The time-honored way is by dry firing. But that doesn't mean just pick up a pistol and start pulling the trigger. No, you grip the weapon correctly while using your best wobble reducing stance. Don't aim at a target. Doing that teaches you to "jerk" when the sight picture is perfect. Dry firing is best done against our wobble grid with a light (laser) and a friend who can help you by coaching. Stare at your front sight and see if it deflects as your hammer drops. Practice. To give your trigger finger a fine education, attach a light or laser sight to your weapon. Sight on and dry fire on our wobble grid in a dimly lit room.

PRACTICE WITH LIGHT LOADS?

Yes. Light loads insure that good shooting habits develop in a new shooter. Shooting heavy loads, especially for novice shooters, often creates the tendency to flinch, jerk, and otherwise avoid recoil.

Dave speaks from combat experience when he says, "During a gunfight, you won't feel recoil or hear the blast. But practice with heavy loads makes you flinch and jerk the trigger so you develop bad habits.

NIGHT SHOOTING

As you know, most of your serious shooting will occur after dark. That's when bad guys come out to do business. Tritium sights enable you to get sight alignment in the dark so you can put a hole in a shadow. Scribbles method of decorating top of barrel also works.

Be careful. Laser sights and lights disclose your position. Moreover, this could be your worst nightmare! You shine a flashlight into a darkened area and discover someone pointing a shotgun at you.

PRACTICE IS REQUIRED

Normally, reloaders are better pistol shots because they can practice without going broke. Whether it costs a lot or a little, you need to practice. You don't need to be great—just better then most. Practice will keep you from placing second in a contest of two.

To be more sure of hitting your target, focus on a small part of the target area. Concentrate on a small spot on the big target and let your hand/eye coordination surprise you. Misses aimed at that tiny area will still hit. *Dave*

DAVID'S TRUE EXPERIENCE

During a fire fight in San Francisco, a perp walked up on a police officer while he was reloading and shot him in the back of the head.

Tragedies like this occur because police officers don't get enough weapons training. Fifty rounds a month is almost minimal. LAPD recommends 80, but PD's don't have the money for ammunition.

We have found a way to train that doesn't cost money. Wobble grid practice.

ADDITIONAL CAUTION

Many a cop owns real property as a result of having tried to render first aid to someone he just shot. That property is in a cemetery. Do not approach downed suspects if you can't see both hands. They'll shoot you for a variety of reasons.

ULTIMATE HANDGUNNER

Chapter 9
Shooting Accuracy:
Three Paths to Shooting Perfection

I traveled to the Shot Show (Shooters, Hunters, etc.) from Kaua'i. Hawaii to talk with manufacturers, huddle with other writers in the press and learn room, and try to see as much as possible from hundreds of people in the business.

"Why are so many guns being sold?" Maybe 26 dead people over a recent weekend in Chicago. Could the recent release of felons from our prisons influence American gun sales? Maybe Obama's purchase of over a billion rounds of ammunition is cause for worry. Finally, think of the influx of all kinds of people from our Southern border.

I met with an interviewed a border patrol agent in Las Vegas during the show. The Border Patrol recently caught an intruder from Poland who could not speak one word of English. What? Why?

How about you? Bought an expensive hand gun? Here's your new problem. It's worthless until you learn to make it do what it was intended for: Bullet placement! Trouble is, it's not a function of the gun. Only you, the shooter, can make this happen.

To create a truly phenomenal shooting result, you need:

1. shooter improvement,
2. gun modification, and
3. ammo improvement.

In other words, learn the ins and outs of handgun shooting. It ain't easy. Actually, it's a discipline. You use major self-disciplines to control trigger, stare at sights correctly, hold the weapon steady and resist the tendency to jerk the trigger and /or flinch when the gun goes "bang!"

Hand load? NO? Then learn the various kinds of ammunition that will enable your gun to perform a wide range of tasks.

We have good news and bad news. The good: We can teach you to hold a handgun so that no "natural" body tension pulls it off to either side. We can teach aiming with proper sight alignment, etc. But the bad news is this: trigger squeeze requires range practice and/or use of our exclusive wobble grid. It's **the vital skill**.

One size fits all. This applies to the manufacture of guns and knives. But a handgun **must** force your trigger finger to pull **straight to the rear!** How can this happen? Gun owner needs to buy custom (size) grips.

Handguns are extremely sensitive to side pressure on a trigger. Especially with short barrels, the slightest sight misalignment will cause a bullet to miss your target completely. Like witchcraft, the sights are aligned and the gun surprises you when it fires. Should be perfect. But it ain't. Why? Your trigger finger did not and could not squeeze directly to the rear.

If you read OUTDOOR KNIFE USE, you know that knife manufacturer's produce knife handles—sized all the same. In other words, one size needs to fit all. Why? Because dealers can't sell big handles to small hands. What does that mean to you? Your knife handle is too small for your hand. Result: A loose (and therefore dangerous) grip. (This is especially true for ladies with long fingernails who stab their own palms with fist closed around a small handle.) If you can't hold on to your knife, you could cut yourself, lose control of the handle at a critical time, or have no way to extract your knife if it gets implanted in something and you can't pull it out.

The above situations and more are good reason to improve your knife's handle so it fits your hand. Actually, that can be good news when you consider all of the outdoor implements you can add to the handle: of course—duct tape, piano wire, parachute cord—and the list goes on. To summarize with regard to knives, you gain utility and safety you can firmly grip the handle with your closed hand (See *OUTDOOR KNIFE USE*, Paul, 3rd Edition).

How about pistols? The grip is a huge deal. If your handgun stock doesnt' fit your hand, accurate bullet placement becomes extremely difficult. You already know that your trigger pull must be **straight to the rear**! To accomplish that on your first shot, your grip must be such around the handle so that your trigger finger is in place on the trigger like a block letter "T." Call the up & down part of the letter the vertical stem. Then the cross at the top must be straight across. The trigger movement must follow the stem precisely, i.e., to the rear. Now, if your **trigger finger is not perfectly perpendicular** (at a 90° angle to the stem) your bullet can follow an Air Force song—"Off we go, into the wild blue yonder..."

It gets worse. After the first shot, the gun recoils! If the handle doesn't fit your hand, the recoil shifts the weapon (even if slightly) so that new grip is different than it was when you first shot. Grip different? Then the trigger finger placement results in new pressures being subtracted from or added to the trigger squeeze. On the range, I have seen some second shots head for the hills. How bad you miss depends on how much your new grip on the weapon has changed.

So new grips on your handgun can make a big difference in accuracy, **provided that** the grips fill your hand enough to enable your trigger finger (the tip of your finger) to touch the trigger **perpendicular to the line of trigger squeeze** and it squeezes straight to the rear.

LEARN TO DETECT WOBBLE

Of all the new concepts and instruction we provide in this book, none is more innovative or important than measuring the amount of natural shake you exhibit when you aim. That's why this book contains THE WOBBLE GRID. You now can measure your shooting variation in MOA (Minutes of Angle). That tells you precisely at what distance you can hit a given size target. The opposite also applies. Excess wobble warns you not to take a distant shot that you know will miss.

You can copy the page on which we drew the graph and work on different handgun shooting positions **while you note how much your wobble varies**. In the past all we had to go by were the bullet holes you made in the target. But <u>the essence</u> of good marksmanship (or any other sport demanding physical performance) <u>is in tracing error to cause</u>. The shape of your shots on our wobble grid helps you to find out why some bullets have a mind of heir own.

What else? You learn trigger control! <u>Almost everybody</u> disturbs sight alignment when the hammer falls. Before the grid, we didn't have a way to <u>measure</u> trigger jerk. Now, as if you could place the whole shooting procedure under a microscope, the wobble grid detects the smallest of variations.

This grid isolates the most frequent causes of poor shooting. Wobble; trigger pull; trigger jerk. Once detected, you can correct them and thus eliminate marksmanship failure.

Finally, anytime you pull your trigger you are attempting to solve particular problems. To be effective, bullets need a certain weight, composition and structure (hollow point, talons, etc). See our chapter entitled *Mix 'n Match*.

Dave test fired a couple of rounds into damp sand. The hand loaded hollow-based wadcutter (reversed with cup forward) expanded to .70 caliber. It out-performed all the factory rounds in expansion. On the right is supposedly the best opener made—the FBI load, a 158 grain lead + P with SWCHP (Semi Wad Cutter Hollow Point) bullet—really no big deal. You can reload 'em better than you can buy 'em.

√ EVERYBODY'S OUTDOOR SURVIVAL GUIDE

More innovations. Teaches exclusive outdoor know-how found nowhere else. Long-range and defensive platform accuracy shooting. Animals for survival. Hand-to-hand combat, water purification, plus a lot more. 120 pp.

√ NEVER GET LOST
(The Green Beret's Compass Course)

Best land navigation system anywhere. Over 55,000 sold. Trash your maps & GPS! Go anywhere, then bee-line back to your starting point without having to back track. System also works equally well in darkness. $8.88

√ CONQUER CRIME!
How to Be Your Own Bodyguard

Book keeps your house un-burgled, your car un-jacked, your child un-abducted, your body un-raped, plus much more. This is the book you can't live without--because without this book, you might not live. Author has appeared on over 250 radio & TV shows. 120 pp. $12.95

The great standard sold through 4 editions. A survival book for modern times that also includes the new and widely accepted concept of neighborhood defense teams. Firearms? YES! They have 17 different attributes listed and evaluated, which makes this the only guide to personalize your gun buying. 120 pp.

Landmark book on new, outdoor knife uses. Outdoor Life Book Club selection. *American Survival Magazine* said, "...16 of the most innovative and informative chapters on knives and knife uses ever written." Just under 40,000 sold. 136 pp.

PATH FINDER PUBLICATIONS
PO Box 1061   Kalaheo, HI 96741
dpaul002@hawaii.rr.com
Booklist: www.survival-books.com

We have gathered information from Navy Seals and Army Special Forces for years to put together the finest survival information anywhere.

BOOKS IN PRINT VERSION: $9.95

Get a FREE sample chapter over the internet.
Get a complete book over the net for price LESS $2.

CONQUER CRIME, How to Be Your Own Bodyguard
NEVER GET LOST   In use by Army Rangers
OUTDOOR KNIFE USE   Over 15,000 in print

GREAT LIVIN IN GRUBBY TIMES
4th Edi, super popular survival .

EVERYBODY'S OUTDOOR SURVIVAL GUIDE
Form a survival team

ULTIMATE HANDGUNNER.
Discover your accuracy @ distance.

ULTIMATE SHOTGUNNER
Mix 'n Match loading for super efficiency

ULTIMATE RIFLEMAN

BE! A SURVIVAL EXPERT.

GLOSSARY

CALIBER. Measurement of bullet diameter, most often in thousandths of an inch.

CONE OF FIRE. Several bullet holes aimed at the same place produces group of holes. Cone of fire is the solid line around the edge of the group. It increases in size as shooter to target distance enlarges.

INDEX. Your personal (never changing) method of holding a handgun so that your trigger finger pulls straight to the rear.

.44 mangl'em. Tribute to Dave's dad, also long-time police officer. He mispronounced magnum deliberately to describe the effect of bullet strikes from a bullet almost half an inch in diameter. Caliber made famous by Dirty Harry (Clint Eastwood classics).

JERK. Shooting no-no. Sudden trigger pull by shooter trying to hit target. Trigger pull needs to be gradual; gun needs to fire as a surprise.

MIX 'N MATCH. Term borrowed from clothing store where a few clothing items can be put together to create a different outfit. Certain bullets perform differently and you need a variety to defends agains different attacks. E.g. distance, barriers to penetrate, and rounds to save you at short distance.

MUZZLE FLASH. Gunpowder still burning after bullet departs from barrel end. Gives away your location at night.

PRESENTATION. Act of bring handgun to bear on target. Best, in our opinion: Inside purse or otherwise hidden, ready to shoot.

SCRIBBLES. Brand name for glow-in-the-dark rubberized (glue?) Untested, but probably is good application for night firing. (Art supply)

SIX O'CLOCK HOLD. Old way of holding just under a bullseye target for visual clarity. Sights are then adjusted to strike the center of bullseye. Replaced by center of mass hold, in which the bullet goes in right on top of the blade (front sight).

SITREP. SITuation REPort. Quick summary usually between to combatants--often armed with firearms.

STANCE. Standing, Sitting, Kneeling or prone. Shooting position in various stances produces more or less wobble as well as reduces your own body exposure to incoming fire.

WOBBLE GRID. Crossed lines for a light to flash on so you can measure aiming deviation (sight bounce) at a distance.